Library of Congress Catalog Card Number 90-90370
ISBN: 0-9627648-1-7

TOP CAT PUBLISHING CO., Post Office Box 309,
Lincroft, New Jersey 07738-0309.

DEDICATION

I dedicate this book to my wife Fern and son Philip. For if it wasn't for them begging me to keep a stray kitten they found in the stairwell of our building, this book would not have been possible.

P.S. We kept the kitten and named her Princess. As of this writing she is 11 years old and still acting like a kitten. A bad one at that, but we love her.

PETS

“Recent census polls state that there are now more than 48 million cats living in the United States.”

"I can't believe it, I dropped a twenty and it's gone."

“Don’t even think about it.”

"OK, who's next?"

NO
PETS
ALLOWED

"Sweetheart did you remember to let the cat in?"

"With a little bit of luck, by the time dessert is served they will have stopped talking about their cat!"

"Hold on dear, Fluffy wants to say hello."

"Can we talk?"

FAMOUS LAST WORDS

"Stop being such a whimp, we can jump twice as far."

"Mom, I found the cat!"

"So, what's so funny?"

"It's not easy living with a witch."

"Sweetheart make sure you stop and buy cat food and kitty litter before you go to work, you know how forgetful you are."

CAT BURGLAR

"Please, just ignore her, she only wants attention."

"I think it will be a long time before Kitty naps on top of the car again."

"I'll be ready in just a moment. Oh, by the way, I hope you like cats."

"Dear, have you seen the cat?"

MOUSE
HUNTING
SEASON
OPENS TODAY

"It's not how loud you meow. The secret is to look sad when you are meowing. Here, now just watch me."

“Wipe that smile off your face and behave yourself tonight.”

"I know you can have them declawed, but do you think there's such a thing as detailing?"

"Talk, talk, talk from morning till night, that's all she does, talks to her pussy cat. Now tell me pal, is that ridiculous or what?"

"Touch one more ball and I'll rip your heart out!"

"It says here that cats sleep approximately 20 hours a day. Edgar! are you listening to me?"

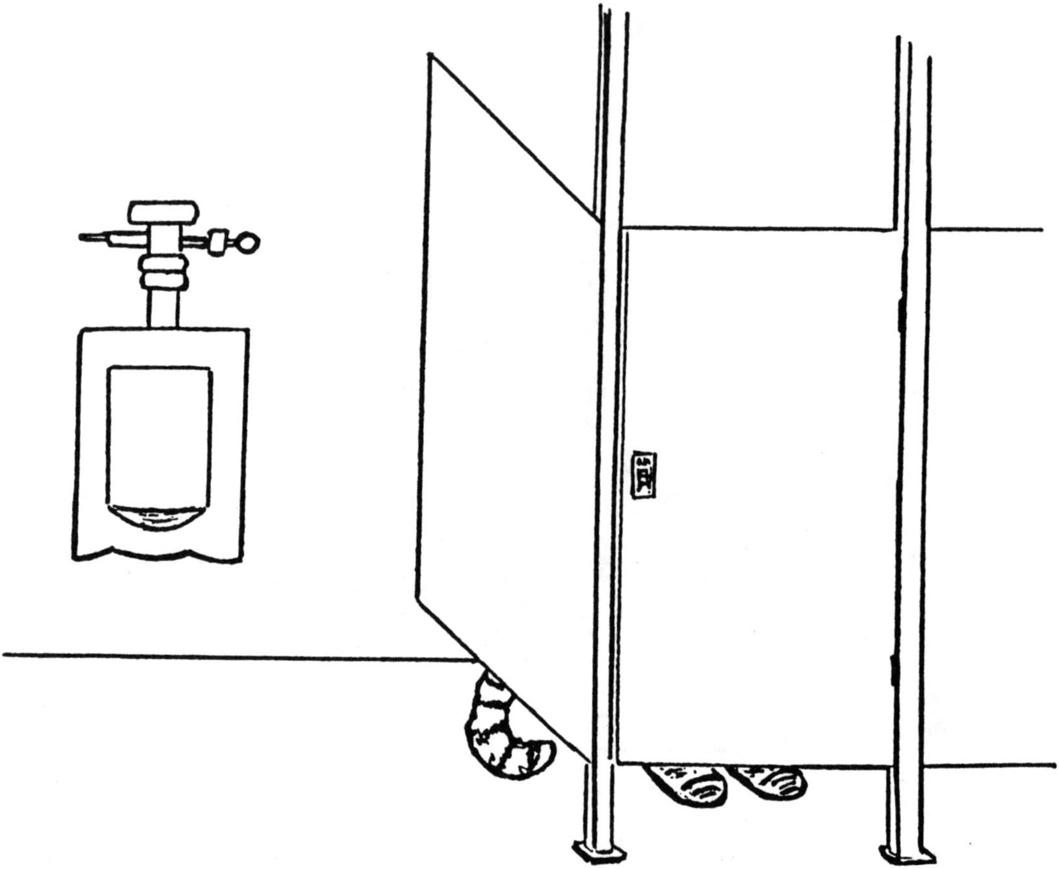

"That's it, this marriage is over, whatever we own we'll split in half."

"Some champion, Mildred tells me that he's still not housebroken."

"Welcome home dear, guess who's back?"

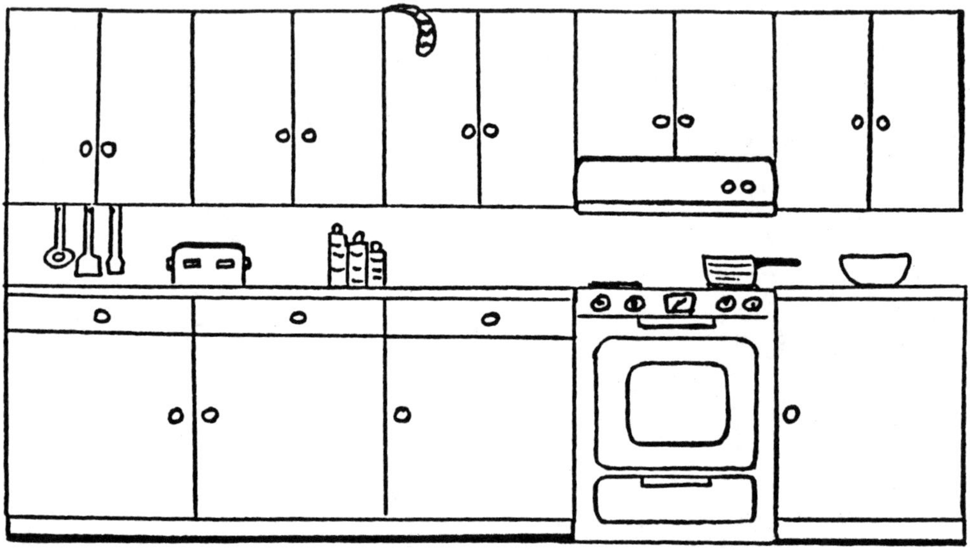

"I love you so much, I don't know what I would do without you!"

"Land sucker, and you're history."

"Now, who ordered the large milk and fish sandwich?"

"I think I'll work on my tan."

"Those students who wish to be excused from today's test, please raise their hands."

1.

2.

"GOT-YA!!"

"Who's next?"

LOOK FAMILIAR

"My mother says we can't have a dog because we're cat people."

“When did you first start noticing these changes?”

"Sweetheart, I said to bring me my hat!"

"See daddy loves it, YUMMY, YUMMY, YUMMY."

WELCOME TO
CAMP-ME-OW

“Boy, this is the life. Fresh air, no master to tell us when to come and go. This is great.”

"He thinks he's so hot!"

"You go on up to bed my dear, Edgar and I are going to have a little chat!"

“Mommy, can I please just keep him till the morning, please?”

"Dogs, Smogs, trust me I know these alleys like the back of my paw."

"Don't look now Mildred, but it looks like you're about to have a hat attack."

"Drop it or learn to swim!"

“This is definitely not going to be a good day!”

HAPPINESS IS

Hanging around the bird feeder.

HAPPINESS IS

Taking the shortcut through your neighbor's yard

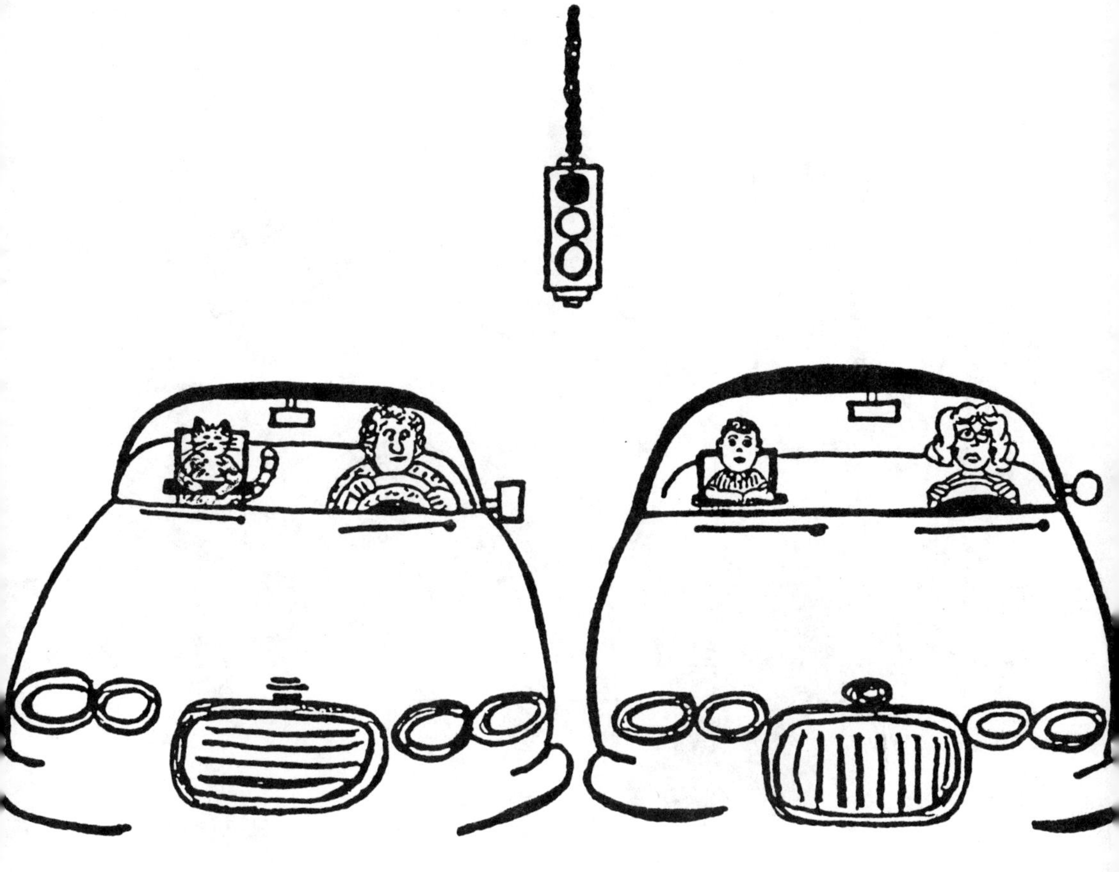

"That's it, you're going on a diet first thing in the morning."

COUNT CATULAR

"Triumphant and proud, the great hunter returns home victorious to share with family members the day's catch."

"Life doesn't get better than this."

“It’s amazing, they do everything together.”

“How come I’m the one that always has to catch him? When do I get my turn?”

“You’ll never guess whose birthday it is today?”

"DROP IT"

“I thought you said your cat didn't scratch.”

"I did, that's not my cat!"

"Poor baby, it's ok, daddy's just had too much coffee to drink today."

ABCDEFGHIJKLMNOPQRSTUVWXYZ
1 2 3 4 5 6 7 8 9 10 11 12 13 14 15 16 17 18 19 20
GOLD FISH
HOW TO CATCH
A MOUSE

"Sweetheart, are you sure you haven't been picking up kitty by the tail?"

"Edgar, where are you? Mommy wants to give you a great big hug."

Z Z Z Z

"Be a sweetheart and let them sit on your chair.
After all this is their favorite show."

"I see you two have been partying again!"

"I just got off the phone with the Vet, he's prescribing a medication for Kitty. We're to give her 6 pills a day for 2 weeks."

"Everyone out, the landlord just left."

HAPPINESS IS

WINTER'S FIRST FIRE

"Darn, that's the third milk cow they've taken this month!"

"This one was taken when she was three months old, and here's one of her at her first birthday party. This one was taken when she came home from the Vets after she was fixed."

"Roger, I'm talking to you. Please answer me. What's the matter, cat's got your tongue?"

"Yes! Yes! George I agree, but just remember there's more than one way to skin a cat."

“Take me to your leader.”

IT'S TUNA TIME"

"And for today's weather, it will continue raining Cats and Dogs for the next few hours."

HOME-SWEET-HOME

"I guess my mother thinks the cat is broken, she keeps telling my dad to have her fixed."

"Kitty has been mad at me ever since I told her you're my best friend."

"I've had better days."

"You're not being fair. You know she won't go to sleep while you're smoking."

"He hasn't been the same since his wife divorced him and received custody of their cat."

FAMOUS LAST WORDS

"It's all in the timing, you see you wait till the last car passes, then you count to three and run."

"I'm back, did you remember to feed the cat?"

"Dinners ready, come out, come out wherever you are."

1.

2.

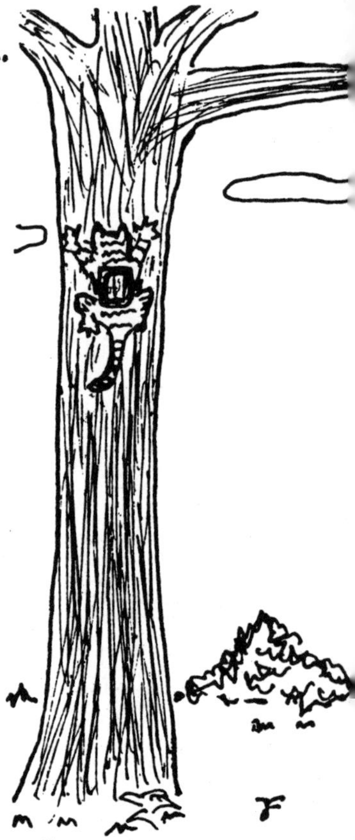

4.

JOE'S FISH SHOP
PIZZA SHOP
MANNYS'
FRESH FISH

"Mr. Cat, I'll see you next."

"MEOW, OUCH! I bet that hurts."

"Here comes that brave Daddy who rescued Mommy's little baby from the big bad tree."

“Go ahead and call your Big brother. I’m so scared,
can’t you see I’m shaking.”

FLUFFYS MILK + CAT NIP BAR
MILK
NO DOGS ALLOWED

10

"Let me guess, you're hungry!"

"Here boy, good boy, that's daddy's little baby pies."

"Helen, you're not going to believe this in a million years!!"

"Do I want a kitten? Lady, what do you think?"

"I can't wait till the girls in my bridge club see this!"

"Do you know how many dogs it takes to change a light bulb? I'll tell you, ten, one to hold the bulb and nine to turn the ladder."

“Everyone say, bye bye Da-Da.”

"Hunting is a lot more fun than I thought it would be!"

CAT T.V.

"We've got good news and bad news Edgar. The good news is Aunt Edna left you all her money. The bad news is when you pass away all the money goes to us."

"Something is not right here. The cat ate all of her food without complaining. She hasn't cried once today to go out and now she's actually lying on your lap purring. I'm telling you I'm sure we let the wrong cat in last night."

“So, I said to her, it’s either me or the cat.”

THE MORNING WAKE UP CALL

"Mom! Mom! wait till you see what we won at Timmy's birthday party."

"You're absolutely sure you want to leave everything to Kitty, and nothing to your children?"

"I'm home!"

JOE'S USED SHOES
JOE'S USED SHOES INC.

"OK, who's responsible?"

"Oops!"

"If you're not off this table in three seconds,
I'll turn you into a tennis racquet."

"Guess whose job it is to let the cat out at night!"

"Be careful, don't fall sweetie."

"Just wait until your father comes home."

"I'm trying, I'm trying."

"Can you imagine there are still some people who believe that if a black cat crosses your path you will have bad luck?"

"Does anyone want ICE CREAM?"

"Children, well not exactly."